KNOWS NO END

Knows No End

Dustin Pickering

Hawakal Publishers

Published by Hawakal Publishers, 185 Kali Temple Road,
Nimta, Kolkata 700049

Email: info@hawakal.com

Website: www.hawakal.com

First edition: August, 2018
Copyright © Dustin Pickering
Cover designed by Bitan Chakraborty

ISBN: 978-93-87883-28-4 (Paperback)

Price: INR 200
US Dollar 7.99

"To be sure, man's search for meaning may arouse inner tension rather than inner equilibrium. However, precisely such tension is an indispensable prerequisite of mental health."—Viktor E. Frankl, *Logotherapy in a Nutshell*

..

..

"However, nature so understood seems to express essence as what underlies a thing's characteristic behavior (for nothing lacks a characteristic behavior), whereas whatness expresses it as underlying the thing's definition, and essence refers to it as that through which and in which a being has existence."—Thomas Aquinas, *De Ente et Essentia*

Vera Ikon
(because to make is to make better)

ACKNOWLEDGEMENTS

Special thanks to Dr. Lucy Wilson for her suggestions on the original manuscript and her inspiring preface. Her insights into the development of the ideas and thought of the work helped me to improve it significantly.

Thank you to Kiriti Sengupta who believes in my work and understands my value in American letters.

A few teachers have inspired me greatly over the years. Mrs. Pat Teltschik and Dr. David Michael Smith deserve a special mention for acting as mentors and pushing me to study more. Without them, my understanding of life would be incomplete.

Finally, my deceased grandmother who remains in my memory as the pillar of who I am. When no one else would raise me, she and her daughter took me in and spoiled me. My experiences in life would not have been as interesting without their care. I spent time on Auburn University's campus and at Shakespeare play rehearsals as a young boy thanks to her. She also guided me with her knowledge of the English language and used her extensive reading experience to come up with suggestions to improve my writings.

Thank you to my uncle and his family—they bought me the computer screen I used to compose this poem. Thank you to my aunt Deborah who is my rock and strength. Her kindness and patience is unsurpassable.

And—the often overlooked source of the eternal truth we seek, God: Your nature we cannot fathom or know, but still we participate in it as your metaphors. We exist in reference to You as subtle analogies. Although we are lost in our preponderant physical abyss and forget the Ultimate, that Being rests within us and we are Its language.

FOREWORD

I sometimes forget that Dustin Pickering is a poet because in my three-year association with him, I am the writer, he is the editor and publisher. Having read his new book of poems, *Knows No End*, I am unlikely to forget again. Dustin has created a twenty-page meditation in several voices, the main one belonging to a woman painter whose chthonic vision of the dead Hyacinth in Apollo's arms ties together all of the poem's important metaphors and motifs:

Apollo knew the power of grief,
how its strength is bold and insuppressible,
and he tilted his friend's head
quietly without asking.

The stillness satisfies me.
Even my heart is still.
It seems once I have ripped
the flesh from the boy flower

I have known the frightful world
for its monstrosity.
Cruelty wears an elephant mask
but behind the simple eyes

is a dark madness, the quenching of life.

In the lines quoted above we can see the poet's remarkable condensation of multiple motifs, including Hyacinth (the spring flower and the ancient myth), love and death, joy and agony. The following lines also reveal Dustin's willingness to ask Big Questions and to answer them with existential insight and the conciseness of England's 17th century Metaphysical poets:

There is nothing beyond my own hunger.
Thoughts are lanterns of my being,
but when sunlight pours upon me
I do not need the horizon.

Divided into four sections, like Vivaldi's *The Four Seasons*, Dustin's poem ties together the changing seasons, the brevity of life, the ubiquity of loss, the question of God's existence, and the role of beauty in the liberation of the human spirit. The poem allows us a glimpse of the poet and artist during their "doubting hours." Their voices mingle, merge and separate, then merge again with questions: "When I smile does eternity know?" "If I sing will the clouds / disappear? If I sing will my flower be disturbed?" The artist responds: "I am free in this solitude. My flower / contains all of Nature's mystery."

In addition to vivid imagery and startling metaphors, Dustin uses short lines and enjambment—especially between stanzas—to keep the poem moving and to infuse this long and sometimes difficult poem with a curious lightness of being. In solitude artist and poet come close to the Hyacinth's insight, but the secret of the "boy flower" is earned, not granted: "The flower will not share its secret," which leads to a crisis of consciousness:

If my thoughts are born from pain,
does this shell of my existence

10

sing like an escaped sparrow
on the wing? How do the trills express grief?

What if I am only a form of thought,
stranded in the dream of another's heart?

[. . .] Capturing essence in the fleeting,
chaotic existence enclosed within Time
is an impossible and dissatisfactory task.

We are reminded that charm and beauty are not sufficient.
We must be willing to step into the Void and reemerge,
like Lucifer, defiant and independent. We must recognize
that "cruelty is who we are: / we are beautiful, terrible
monsters" who must own our fear and sorrow. Poet and
painter must look within because, as Imagine Dragons
sings: "That's where my demons lie."

Lucy Wilson, PhD
Professor Emerita, Loyola Marymount University

OPENING NOTE

"Can I see anothers woe,
and not be in sorrow too."

William Blake, "On Anothers Sorrow"

The idea for this poetry collection occurred spontaneously during a text conversation with a friend. That friend, my business partner Z. M. Wise, sought relationship advice from me (of all people) and I began proposing ideas for poems out of the blue. A mutual friend, Houston model and artist Vera Ikon, became the central "character" of the collection after I joked that someone should be painting a flower in the poems.

Z. M. allowed me to run with my own idea as it developed into something more elaborate and serious.

I first met Vera Ikon at ArtCrawl, downtown Houston. She was showcasing her paintings themed with stigmata and anime symbolism. I thought her paintings were interesting and we eventually used one for a cover of *Harbinger Asylum* in Spring 2015 and again in Spring 2017. I have met with Vera only once since that day and we exchanged messages and texts from time to time.

For personal reasons, I felt she deserved to have this collection dedicated to her. The theme presented is humankind's struggle to know and understand truth, to liberate the human spirit, and to find beauty through cold suffering. An artist of any kind will tell you doubt is a cruel master, but it is one of those things essential to the search for meaning.

Dustin Pickering
Houston, Texas

FIRST MOMENTS

Sometimes a meadow is a place of grace.

Wandering, I carry my brushes
until I reach a quaint hill.
This will be my resting space.

I lay my head on the dewy grass
and as I fall asleep I already dream,
this dream is of the most beautiful man.
His face emanates the kindest light
like Apollo who also dreams.

When I awake, my tears remind me
of my loneliness.
My heart aches and I hold my hand close
to remind it that a dream is not an isolated thing.

My easel sits above my head, proud

and irreproachable.
Like a patient spider, it rests in its nest
and waits for my hand to find inspiration.

The night does not whisper.
The wind is a mild friend,
visiting at my doubting hours.
I sit. I wait. The heart in me

seems impatient. I know myself well.
I cannot decide if I am thrilled to be alive
or if my agony is too surreal to cut open
for evaluation. My thoughts, tender and quiet.

The dreams I experience are vanishing realities.
My imagination plays at having captured
the pearl of universal longing,
at knowing the sacred truth of pain.

What is blood? What is my own breath?
Do I shun tenderness or do I wait?
A touch is before me, the sunlight reaches
to me like veins of compassion.

If I weren't alive, I would not know the solitude
I only appreciate when I am face-to-face with others.
If I lived in a castle of tears,
my longing would not mean less.

My eyes open upon the field before me.

Empty serenity stands like a majestic oak.
Though the light surrounds me wherever I may reach,
I still feel the cold desperation of fear and uncertainty.

I have a can of brushes beside me,
some thickened with yesterday's paint.
I do not always wash the signs of the past away.
They are my symbols. They make my eyes beam.

I loved once but the man I knew
was only the shell of a man.
Desire faded like an expression on a photo
From years past. I danced and I kissed,

yet the abundance of tears made my sighs
trivial and small. I left the soul of that man,
my lover and friend, in the dark envy
of forbidden mystery.

Men would never see me as real.
They looked at me as flesh,
thought of me as a photo or empty head,
but my creations knew me

and they smiled at my strokes.
I smiled back, knowing that the dreams
I experienced became real
in such a way as not to hurt me.

SUMMER

Sometimes a kiss is more than lips

wanting to touch.
When I know a kiss, the stranger I embrace
becomes a vision and I withdraw quietly.

My hand feels the longing toward creation.
I reach for my brushes and palatte.
As I bend down, I notice a quiet, tender flower
lifting its head to my smile.

Who is this? My dream? Does this solitude
suddenly awaken without me?
I touch the tender petals as it shies from my gestures.
It is a lovely hyacinth, flower of sacrifice.

Why do you retreat from my call?
My spirit is a kiss through castle windows,
Tears of unfulfilled longing withstood.
I may have offended your repose,

but I promise friendship.
I will not pluck you from your roots
like the world that raped me, pleased at my helplessness.
Heart! What do the dreamers and lovers wish!

My thoughts become tender and sweet.
This flower is my passion,
and passion is the fruit of my art.
Hyacinth, know I am tender!

I want to peer into the eternity of this flower!

I want to know its heart.
My fingers cannot awaken its slumber,
but my brushes will interpret its rest.

Warm breezes fill me with hope.
My flower smiles at the delight
expressed in my movements.
What, is Nature bliss? Is this moment

mine or does it belong to God?
If this hour has no one to possess it,
then how am I to make it real?
Only hours, not empires, can be held.

My mind is tranquil but the seasons move fast.
This is only a passing fantasy, as moments drift.
If I try to hold it in rapture,
will I ever know the next moment?

How can I grasp the singleness
of this trysting torch, my liberty,
without offending Time and existence?
When I smile, does Eternity know?

An endless question can only tempt

with answers. How did I find myself here?
This meadow is clear enough
to see the open sky, and release my heart.

I am free in this solitude. My flower
contains all of Nature's mystery,
fragments of sympathy and joy.
Studying singularities, my hand quietly adds to the canvas.

I will bring sadness and glory from
the depths of Hyacinth, his face the wounds
I've experienced, while I ease my own throbbing
emptiness. What is inside the heart is unknown,
completely.

My brush will awaken the mystery.
The light strokes of the brush hairs
have their own language.
I am their interpreter and translator.

Each motion is a heartbeat,
and my quietude of soul tells me
this work is good. The world becomes
my angel, my river of song.

Rain cannot disturb me. Painting is immortal,

and the love within will make it bright.
Clouds develop above me,
but I cannot stop because this fury possesses me.

Fury is gentle in my brushes. They are made
from fine horsehairs. If I sing, will the clouds
disappear? If I sing, will my flower be disturbed?
Hyacinth knows his own song.

Perhaps my eyes are dimming
and I am returning to dream.
I feel the aching in my heart
but my hand continues to move,

and I bend my back in breathlessness.
I try to hold myself up,
but the moment is too heavy.
I close my eyes and succumb to the dark.

FALL

A mild darkness sets in overhead.

Still, I feel the tenderness of hope
through me like a bolt of lightning
slightly out of reach.

A change of season taught me one thing.
Capturing essence is only done
by freezing and examining moments like photographs.
Such a gift, perhaps, is only for the dead.

As I painted my flower, the winds
wept coldly. I reached across the easel
and tilted it back to get a clearer impression
of what my hands created.

Night comes soon but inner lamps
keep me company and I will
rest in evening's lap.
My heart will know sadness and grief, yet kindness.

I am reminded of my first teacher,

his sharp intellect and eye
instructed me to cease repetitions
and craft the image meaningfully.

Reconstruct it several times
before considering it complete.
He told me, "The art of perfecting an image
is often misunderstood—

amateurs think careful thought
and planning prepares
exact beauty.
But no, the truth appears through abundance."

I understood this advice
when I could not mix my preferred palette
and my painting stared dully back,
refusing to come alive…then I developed patience.

Try, then try again. Don't be ashamed
of your foolishness. Tears and blood
are constantly replenished, and the persistence
of pain does not make you a failure.

This is one miracle I fathom
in my concentration:
that I create, ex nihilo, the essence
of one beauty, one fire of Time.

I lie down in the grass to rest.

Small droplets of rain come
from the heights
and are warm on my body.

I reach my arms across the grass
and feel the roundness of the hill,
experiencing earth in its nurture.
My flower has turned its petals inward

like a monk, softly dreaming of the dark.
Something about darkness reminds
me of the womb; I almost feel an aloneness
of birth in the perplexed silence.

I open my eyes, afraid, and feel
an uncomfortable immediacy;
something groping and violating my solitude.
My eyes lash in fury.

I am blinded by the black density
That makes me heavy.
I push myself up, stand abruptly,
and search for the stars penetrating

the sky at night. There is a fog before me,
and stumbling I stare, finally catching
a haze of moonlight.
Silently my heart thinks, "Again. Again."

In the morning, my mood insists I rise

for the clamoring of birds.
Sunlight, delightfully crisp,
fills the meadow like a dream.

Tiny birds pounce and dance
in the grass while I stretch my arms upward.
They are not disturbed by my motions.
A smile tickles the edges of my mouth.

Warm blood circulates through my body,
and I pick up my brushes to paint...
again, my Hyacinth is quiet, motionless,
closed and private, not wishing for sympathy.

The season must make me wonder.
I clean my brush and carefully trace
the flower's grace in the air,
before I begin painting.

Within moments I begin to draft my image,
reflecting on the source
of all that is good and delightful
This nameless Nothingness,

impersonal and luminous, allows me
to judge my own flourishes.
Its animal emptiness, full of passion
and fear, is friend to those in solitude.

Is this Something an endless dream?

Am I, as flesh and body, a formless waste
like the deeps? Do the birds know
the force of my being?

Silent, still as a photograph,
the flower's beauty carries my soul
to compunction and dreariness.
I do not sense life within it—

And could not make what lives
Move to my memory's influence.
The Hyacinth is stretched by root
into the same ground my feet rest upon.

Quick brush strokes, still no
enviable design. Nothing. My heart too is empty,
dry as a fallen leaf, and my will is wasted
on this fruitless attempt to *understand*.

An act of creation isn't simply imitation.
An artist wants to assure possibilities,
to delve into the heart of things.
If she doesn't return from the darkness,

Perhaps she will be forgotten.
Like a mermaid, enchanting sailors with her voice,
she dives deeper into the sea, leaving mystery
in her rippled wake.

However, her enchantment so dazzles
that its absence is not recognized

by their senses. The young mermaid, deep underwater,
leaves an impression that cannot be unlearned.

The sailors feel an invisible serenity
The mermaid's song attunes their understanding to truth.
Sometimes forgetting is a blessing—
being unconscious intimately inspires.

I still wonder if my flower will wither,

if it will guard its secrets by pulling inward
again and again as it has before.
How do I know its mystery, infinite and reluctant?

Is there a way to share its pleasant ambivalence?
When I look deeply, its smile has no life.
Something empty and dark encloses its flesh.
Timorous petals spotted with blood.

It digs itself into the ground
seeking its own meaning.
Quietly, it attains what all living beings desire:
Security with passion, adventure through sense of self.

Yet the petals fold, neither ashamed nor modest,
and my dance summons only
an intimate ambiguity.
When I reflect on myself I feel like a fool,

some jester in a lawless court
who fears for his own head.
My Hyacinth, sweet dreamer and sacrifice
from Time's wounds, I wonder if you are truly alive?

I begin to paint again. I add splotches of violet,

some crimson, and try to capture the light.
My concentration seeps in the workings of my flower,
and I remember my first discovery of it fondly.

Like a child taking steps away from Mother,
I reach down and my hand
Encounters tender softness.
My surprise at this discovery fills my eyes.

A moment's pause, then a sigh.
Nothing could inspire so greatly
as this tender, quiet thing!
Something so mysterious, so attractive,

so genuine, could not be forgotten.
Immortal hands framed this flower,
decorating it with dolor and divinity,
and my amazement is not enough worship.

Its sweet innocence,
like the troubles of youth,
fill me with awe and pity.
It breathes splendor, flower of sacrifice!

Stillness imposes a hush over my heart.

In this moment, I feel most intimate
with Hyacinth. His youthful glances
like curtains opening to the daylight.

I could not be happier.
The breeze lightly tosses my hair
like a small fairy passing through.
The grasses rock to and fro

in cheerful worship.
I am not easily disturbed in my focus
because I am within this snapshot
of eternity's imagination,

looking through the double gaze
of the cosmic mirror.
Now I approach the memories
of my mind, dreaming elegantly.

Some moments create new faces
in the landscape, and others
make the silence weep.
I will not succumb to my own fascination.

I breathe, close my eyes, open them slowly.
I look again at what my hand has done,
and my imagination delights
at the colorful skill my hours unfolded.

Yet it doesn't reach deep enough,
and I find that what it says

is only part of what is really said.
How do I pull the essence from this romance?

The flower shyly closes its eyes.
Seeming to know what I seek,
the Hyacinth protects its interior
but playfully suggests answers.

Am I falling in love?

Is love some sort of knowledge
that only the lonely seek?
What am I in my hiddenness?

Is there a fearful darkness
in the surrounding skies?
Even if I see the bright lore
of life's blessedness,

do I know it as real?
How do I know the reality
if I do not know the ideal splendor?
If transcendence is external to this,

do I declare my eyes open,
do I reach higher?
The mystery deepens in my solitude.
The flower will not share its secret.

How do these things grow, wither,
die, return?
If I become what I admire,
will I know it fully?

Is beauty something that inhabits
or is it a quality of touch,
a sensation of immortality?
Why lust when the truth speaks?

I don't understand. I cannot see.
Something is growing cold

beside me while I reflect on the Spring.
I awake to white crystals flaking on the ground.

WINTER

The sky is insolently clear,

and the ground covered with flakes
of snow. My flower sings his beauty strong above
the cold blanket of frost.

Still I know of the living death.
My limbs feel frozen,
so I test my cheeks for warmth.
The night comes slowly.

When the stars peer down
perhaps I will not shiver
so much even though
there is nothing to fear.

The frozen winter is part
of Nature's mourning,
but what is she mourning?
Is there a cloud of dreams above?

Will something speak after
we have spoken?
I reach for my brushes again.
The can is cold, and each brush

blanketed in snow.
I am reminded of flesh
and its softness. When does
warmth leave the blood?

I sense butterflies of yearning within me.
I want to fall asleep forever
or wake in a cocoon,
and the winter snow tries to fulfill me.

If my thoughts are born from pain,

does this shell of my existence
sing like an escaped sparrow
on the wing? How do the trills express grief?

What if I am only a form of thought,
stranded in the dream of another's heart?
Does his heart grow in tenderness
or does it bleed in the wind?

I could float or I could climb the heights,
looking for the lost angels of truth.
If I sink into laughter,
remind me there are no tales

to imagine in the dark.
A silence overcomes the meadow
when I think on the ultimate vision,
as if shadows were sharpening their teeth.

I face the hours reluctantly.
The couriers of night have not visited
this empty lot where I rest my head.
After brief interlude, I return to painting.

I use my fingers to dry the snow

from the brush.
My fingertips redden in the moment,
and after shaking the cold water

from them I hold them together
to return them to warmth.
I gingerly grasp the brush.
As I paint, I am reminded

of the reason I began my art.
Capturing essence in the fleeting,
chaotic existence enclosed within Time
is an impossible and dissatisfying task.

My veins are not immortal
and I cannot strain my hours
to search for the core
behind emptiness.

If Nature is truth and there is some

Forgotten friendship between myself and her,
my attempts to recreate her light
will reunite our hearts.

If night is the veil over my eyes,
a hot mist will melt my thoughts
and drive me forward in paradigms
of utter abandon; I will forgive.

Heart's kite in the sky making wind
its own father of delight,
my radiance, the sighs of sweet mercy,
the fever and ecstasy of creating again.

I am the dream someone experiences
in this cold imbecility;
my hand reaches out for the lonely sky
to find the mystery of being born.

Born, remembered, the rebirth of recollection:
I only sense Truth, but it is not my form.
I capture senselessness because I am shadow.
Night is chaos thrust into my yearning, causing me to
forget.

My veil is crystal; the snow is memory

becoming wet and dark.
If art is my pain and exultation,
I must breathe life into this painting.

It must come alive! The frenzy
of my tightened hands in motion,
brush turning fire in the winter,
these magic minarets erected from my mind!

Each application of pigment is a stretch
closer to truth. If I reach far enough,
my arm will bridge Spirit and Earth.
I am the Mother of sea and star,

and my thought burns unity from the blood.
Rapture is within me—it penetrates my heart subtly.
I grip my most tender parts as my eyes fill with light.
I am born to remember.

A form is a passage in time's dream.
Joy is my miracle as I face the flash
of my existence, like a photograph in fire.
Everything burns.

If only the Hyacinth were a boy,

a young man with bright eyes
and glowing skin,
I would never want to die again.

Some rumors are true.
I am deeply in love with his magic.
The quiet psalm of his soul
guides my eyes as I paint.

Light and dark embody the lust of existence—
Twins of our solemn screaming, they devour
one another contentedly. I won't let the ghosts
of ancient eras silence me.

I am one, to become, the shadow of Antiquity,
my face fills with blushing.
It is not shame that taints me
but the love of the music

only I hear, the song of envy.
If Pan were not alone, his flute
would delight the nymphs
who flee his solitude.

I have you, delicate flower,

to invite my abundance.
Treasures are sometimes bright and becoming,
but the greatest gifts are hidden.

If my eyes do not see glory
in what is truly sweet,
perhaps it is my own sense of darkness
that blinds me to golden power.

Only once in each meager life
does some glowing sacrifice empty
into the aching soul—
to make blossom what is deep.

Love, if charm and beauty alone,
is a toy and not worth the adventure.
I must feel mercy's thick foot
fix me down as I am stretched taut

across the horizon of guilt,
black boot and fear,
and all the pride of the world.
Dalliance with evil is bittersweet.

Cruelty is a flesh-like thing,
stinging the stainless body
of a child, killing the sour race
of an offense we ourselves yearned for.

If separation is what defines Sin,
the angels know my defiance and division

and how I fought for independence
from the insolence of the venomous God.

I cannot fly from existence.
I must face it with outstanding grace,
and look vehemently at the Void
where this struggle began,

both the forceful Creator's and my own.
This cruelty is who we are:
we are beautiful, terrible monsters
seeking the precious dawn of our lips.
If I knew the moon and felt its reluctant
glow like a razor against a man's face,
perhaps my soul, my enemy, would whimper
and become dust swirling in the meadow.

But since I am the quiet one, the tempestuous one,
my own rage is the blaze of heart,
the sacrifice of one thousand flames
reaching into the burning symbols of Time.

As I contemplate the forms of Truth,
engaging in the battle tough with turbulence,
I feel the winter receding,
and I know the return of seasons.

When a year begins fresh after long serenades
in snow, delight announces the bright resurrection;
our human faces are struck with warmth
like a trembling hand plucking a guitar.

The song grew quiet and cold, pausing in its deepness.

There are moments when music must reflect on itself before it moves forward. When night becomes crimson, a distant clock utters the coming friendships.

SPRING

"While he held him the boy's head fell back as a flower does when its stem is broken."

—Edith Hamilton, *Mythology*

As if joy and hope were my only possessions,

I waited for the sun to open its petals
against the hapless sky waiting
for its proud proclamation.

What do the Furies tell in this calm night?
Does Apollo, god of sorrows now unfolding,
know the jealousy of the wild West Wind?
If this youth is so beautiful as to inspire

ruthless insolence of sacrifice,
why shouldn't he be immortal?
Hyacinth, dream child of my awakening,
the spring shines its delight to your eyes.

"Alas" drawn on your petals, my flower,
now I know why you have been my companion
in these rustic days, tired and old.
These intense months, now passed, have caused

tear after tear in my heart.
I drift my hand across your white petals,
voicing the blood of your sacrifice
like a child imitating his father.

The frenzy of my hand,
as wind thrusting the discus
toward your soft forehead,
creating death from its silence.

The Sun was a dreamer in fallen days

when our hands were thick
around one another like Medusa vines
freezing faces into stone.

Now alive, the Sun has revealed the secret
of my sorrow; suddenly, I am kept awake
by the harrowing of animals in my soul
and I do not know my own world.

If I ask Apollo, he will try to court me
like the wound brought by the West Wind,
and I already know well his assignment.
I do not bleed to hear sparrows besides.

Whatever I sought in compunction
I already found in the grief
of this child, blood spilled into the earth.
Hyacinth, of the days I have adored you

this final moment is my rest.
On the ground I weep,
waiting for life's renewal
at the threshold.

If a flower has opened life's majesty
through the palm of my creation,
does this reveal my own sagacious thrust
as I ponder and paint?

Apollo knew the power of grief,
how its strength is bold and insuppressible,

and he tilted his friend's head
quietly without asking.

The stillness satisfies me.

Even my heart is still.
It seems once I have ripped
the flesh from the boy flower,

I have known the frightful world
for its monstrosity.
Cruelty wears an elephant mask
but behind the simple eyes

is a dark madness, the quenching of life.
Hideous shriveled faces cower
in the houseless abyss.
Names are kept under like a flood.

Bones are omens from the trembling
hands of God, who delves in ancient secrecy
to display His hoax.
If Memory is the face after the dark

and madness is the Spring of our lives,
we will sink into mayhem with each loss.
Wisdom is the world's law and fear,
but as I learn to see I also learn to forget.

There is nothing beyond my own hunger.
Thoughts are lanterns of my being,
but when sunlight pours upon me
I do not need the horizon.

This is eternal doubt: to live.

My restless mind examines each shadowy splendor
and synthesizes, suppresses the thought,
and makes what is before me anew.

To make is to make better.
I try, in spite of tears and bitterness,
to find hope and heart in tiny things.
Somehow he, the flower, became my eye.

If I look to the light, blindness overcomes
my vision and dreams dance like a storm.
The illusion is in waking.
There wasn't a truth in this flower.

The Hyacinth, poor bleeding thing,
is a young and quiet child
of Nature's secrecy. If I am to love,
must I know the truth?

Is love too an illusion? Is my heartbeat
merely sensation, something external
to my own existence?
Fortitude teaches me

that intense pain and doubt are chained
as prisoners in the dark.
I surrender the unique work created
by my hands to You.

You are secret bliss:
open the flower
and show us the tears
instilled in Creation.

www.ingramcontent.com/pod-product-compliance
Lightning Source LLC
Chambersburg PA
CBHW021147020426
42331CB00005B/937